For You and not for You

R. G. Morey

ISBN 978-93-5438-948-1
© R. G. Morey 2021
Published in India 2021 by Pencil

A brand of
One Point Six Technologies Pvt. Ltd.
123, Building J2, Shram Seva Premises,
Wadala Truck Terminal, Wadala (E)
Mumbai 400037, Maharashtra, INDIA
E connect@thepencilapp.com
W www.thepencilapp.com

CONTENTS

I saw the sun

I saw the sun, I was happy
I saw the flowers, I sang
I saw the river, I swam
I saw the ice cream store just opened, I ran

There was a boy I loved
Worked there his days were rough
But I knew him he was brave, boy he was tough
I saw him there getting ready and I was happy

Those blue eyes, that sweet smile
His way to greet me was special
His way to look at me was special
He was lost in his job, but outside in the park, I was his
and he was mine
He was my special

He held me one day, pulled me closer
He closed the shop, held me tight
He kissed me, I kissed him, I knew it was right
He had to leave the town he said, and we had our first
fight

I saw the sun, I was happy
I saw the flowers, I sang

I saw the river, I swam
I saw the ice cream store just opened, I ran

But there he was not

Drinking

I was in the bar, drinking ad thinking
Thought of you for a minute, thought what will you think
of my drinking
Will you like it, a muscular hobby or hate it, a disgraceful
liking
I was indeed not at all just thinking of you, not that I love
you, I thought of fighting as well

I got up from there, was bore and tired, unwilling to go
home
There was nothing and no one in there for me to be with
I thought of you again for some reason, for some reason I
wanted to call you
And ask you, if everything was alright and could I come
over, and who you are with

Drunk I was so just jumped on my bed
Thinking of you again, I had a dream, I was with you
You were with me, I was smiling, you were happy, I held
you close, you pulled me closer, I kissed you, you loved me
Next morning, I was going to see you And that was the
relief

I would have you at least for a few hours
For some reason I think you are lonely and love me

For some reason I think, you are something else, a magnet with amazing power

My Heart

I see the girl smiling
I see her dance
I see her walking
I see her stealing my heart
My heart
My heart
My girl stole my heart
My baby stole my heart

She kept me smiling
She kept me happy
She was the charm
She kept me fighting

and I and I and l lost my heart
I lost my heart to an angle
My girl stole my heart

My heart
My heart
My girl stole my heart
My dear baby, stole my heart

Out of this town
Out of this city

Lets get out
Of this life of pity
Live away far away
Together we will be
Together we will be
Oh!!!
I want to see you baby
I want to see you dance
I want to keep you with me
Cause

You stole my heart!!!!!!
You stole
You stole my heart!!!!!

My heart
My heart
My girl stole my heart
My baby stole my heart

Let me Die

Let me die, let me be
Leave me there let me see
Let me go let me live
Let the world run let me chill

Let me dance
Come with me
Lets go together
Lets all be free

Let me sing
The song I like
Let me have my moments
Let me have my life

Let me dance
Come with me
Lets go together
Lets all be free

I know you have dreams too
There is wish to fly in you
Don't force your soul to be trapped
Not let go of my hand
And I will take you with me

The place I know you want to see
Lets be together
Lets be free
Don't be afraid my friend
This is our chance
Hold my hand forget the world be free
Lets be free

Let me dance
Come with me
Lets go together
Lets all be free

Fate

Let me tell you something
Before it is too late
I wanted to be with you
But this fate!

Can I ask why you changed
You are happy I think
I would have not asked, my dear
But my heart is caged

Hero I am not, I am sorry
My love
If I were the person you admire
Then you had not changed I know

Sick as I am
Can't change the fate
Life is shortening each moment
I wanted to tell you even when I know I am too late

Let that smile o yours
Come back
Dance again don't have to hide behind
That mask
Anymore

Life seems empty without you
Maybe that is why god is taking it away
It is a moment of joy
Now that I will be out of your way

Party

Let's go to the party
Let's go to the beach
Let's go to the river
Let's go lets go lets go

There we will play
There we will dance
There we will sing
There we will dance
There we dance

Sun is shining
It's calling us to play
Flowers are dancing in the garden of life
It's calling us to be free

There we will play
There we will dance
There we will sing
There we will dance
There we dance

Let it be
Let it be
Let it be

Let it go, lets go
Lets go to the beach
Lets go to the heaven

I want to smile again
 I want you to be with me
I want to live again
I want you to be with me

We will be friends
We will go to the beach
Together
There we will play
There we will dance
There we sing
There we will dance
There we dance

Oh my friend
We will, my friend
We will go to the party
We will go to the beach
We will dance together
We will, we will
Oh!!!!!!!
Lets go!!!

We Stole

We stole we stole
We stole and we won
We had we had
We had and we lost

There was a white sky
There was a river of clean water
There were flowers and trees
There is now nothing
Nothing to be seen

Air used be pure
Water was sweet
We loved one another
We loved the earth

There was a white sky
There was a river of clean water
There were flowers and trees
There no nothing
Nothing to be seen

Hey human I ask you
Why did you ignore
Why I ask? Why? Would you let me die

Couldn't you hear my screams
Couldn't you hear my screams

Why you are lying to your children
Why you are lying to yourself
Why you have to go ahead in life
That you have to cut your roots off

There was a white sky
There was a river of clean water
There is now nothing
Nothing to be seen

There was a white sky
There was a river of clean water
There is now nothing
Nothing to be seen

Should have

You should have stayed
You should have stayed
 I wanted say that I love you
I wanted to say that I miss you

You should have stayed
You should have stayed
Out of this dead world I had chosen you as my one
I wanted to tell you that you have me

Long ago, once in night, I had held you hand
Once long ago, I had written your name in the sand
Long ago I had your hand in my hand
Long ago I had smelt your perfume to close

You should have stayed
You should have stayed
I wanted to say that I love you
I wanted to say that I miss you

I had many things to say
I had thought of thousand new ways
To meet you, to kiss you, to take you a dance, to see you
have your laugh
Oh girl!

I love you, and that's is what I know
You should have stayed
You should have stayed
I wanted to tell you that I love you
I wanted to tell you that I miss you

The Ripper

Ripper of the souls

Walked on earth

Amongst all mortals

To get the ones whose time has come

A mortal child

Innocent fibble

World to him is his mother still

His soul Ripper takes with no regrets

A man killed so many

Now his time has came

He is cold and weak

His soul ripper pull out with one hand

A woman on a path

Laying in her own blood

Mortals crying, mortals talking, mortals laughing

He takes her soul out gently

An old man on a soft bed

Saw the ripper coming and smiled

Finally, his time had come

Ripper extend a hand for the old man to hold

Ripper took all souls and carried them with him

In one bag he keeps them

All mortal differences and hates he did not let them carry

Ripper walks amongst mortal to collect souls

She waits

Ghostly sky sallow moonlight

Red roads dark shadows

Howling trees mourning night

He she hates, there she waits

Empty eyes bloody mouth

Stomach full of worms burnt half face

She cries and laughs in squeaky tone loud

He, she hates, there she waits

One day he comes slowly in dark

Sees her in blood shocked white

stare at the ghost and laughs

He, she hates and there she waits

One day he comes slowly in dark

Sees her in blood shocked white

stare at the ghost and laughs

He, she hates and there she waits

Walk away passed through her

She tries to strangle to hold to kill

like life there was no power given to her

He, she hates and there she waits

Empty eyes bloody mouth

Stomach full of worms burnt half face

She cries and laughs in squeaky tone loud

He, she hates, there she waits

Love

Ghost came into my room

Said my time was coming soon

I wasn't scared, it was a girl

I knew it wasn't my time yet, that goon

Her face was cut in the middle

There a bunch of hair in the right hand

A person's ear in her left

Her feet were dirty covered in sand

I took my blanket over my head

And slept like a child

She pulled my blanket away and screamed

Her hairs were standing her jaw fallen

I put fingers in my ears and dreamed

Her long nail hand she put on my face

With other, she pulled my hair up

Now that I knew it was serious I got out

I tried to pull her hair, but, no luck

When I was out of the bed finally

She groaned at me in hate

Then she lay down on the bed and asked for a blanket

I slept on the couch as it was too late

Before she said, good night

She smiled in delight

And I could still get a priest

But I won't, all couples fight

Song

The song she sang

The way she danced

Her screams her tears her bloody face

Is still fresh in my memories

The book she used to read

Me laying on her lap

She running with one bad leg

Is still fresh in my memories

Her figths with me

when she wouldn't speak

Her last cry for help

Is still fresh in my memories

She never wished to be mine

Not till that night

When she was lost to all

And found by me

Her begging her prayers

The way she used to lie

Her body laying in my cage

Is still fresh in my memories

Police questioning to me

World crying for her, her face on TV

My envy for her

Is still fresh in my memories

Nothing for me

The dark and warm

Cold and bright

Night that was unforgettable

Is now lost in memories

Far and soft

Rough and close

Your touch meant to be for me

Is now not anymore

Death and hope

Dispair and life

Meaning of all this we defined once

Is now nothing for me

Me and you

You and me

True you and true me, truth in us

Is now as false as current government's promises

Truth

Blood covered her face

And flesh stuck in her nails

Her hair burnt dry thin

eyes dripping red and face pail

She is trying to speak

Her teeth are broken

Her tongue pulled out

She could not tell where she was taken

It was night when she was found

Her blood all around

Laying in mud

Crying on that ground

Her mother cried

No one stood with her

No one wrote her complain

No one fought for her

The girl died

Like they always do

No one noticed

No one knows she was who

Burnt girl was then forgotten

Even by her mother

No one cared or shed a tear when

There come new body and then another

Flowers

Small and big flowers

Shining in sun scattering their beauty

You and I stood far, always then, together

And when I reached, alone, the land was gone

The lake we used to drink from

Water purest and cold and warm

You and I used to play barefoot

And now water is gone

White sky with so many shaped clouds

Birds flew singing passionately lullabies

You and I used to lay down on grass that hides underneath concrete now

But the sky is not white any more and I miss you

When I used to cry

You always ran to me

But now I can't see you

And you are gone, like everything else I loved

The deep forest and families of creatures

The flowing river and fresh rain

My family, my friends, my home, good food

And you are gone, like everything else I loved

Now I am crying again

But you are not here by my side to hold my hand

I can't breathe and the woman says, I will meet you soon

I am happy, but the pain won't let me smile

The sky is dark, darker than most morning

The wind is dustier, dustier than most days

The woman says, you have fresh air and good food, but I
know you haven't eaten

You are waiting for me, like you used to do

Pain and Darkness

Into the hell

Through the carrier of deaths

I travel

Moaning in pain

Out I see cannot

Eyes are bleeding

And darkness drank me in

Blood I drink, rotting flesh, is all I got

And now the flesh

I hinged to for so long

Will be part of the darkness

I will be lost in madness maze

I hear them

Part I cannot

They have rotting flesh and stinky blood

But their pain is not the same

The carrier will stop

And the end will be pleasing

Till the horror begins

And like my blood and flesh, my soul starts to rot

Me and you

Look the sky is falling

Look the floor is shaking

Look the life is funny, see me laugh

Look the wall is moving, still can't touch

Was that mine or yours

Was she mine ever, or it was a game

Was not that trip the best

Was not I your best friend then

It is empty again, who drank

It is raining I think, Nah! Maybe!?

It is her fault, not mine, you know

It is you who keep me happy man, give me a kiss

Find, I am done anyways

Fine, I am never going to meet her anyways

Fine, I am ready, where are we going

Fine, lets dance

Children

It was a good morning for child

It was a morning for child

It was beginning of misery for child

It was day of hunger for child

Child woke up and had a blast, played and danced a lot

Child woken up by screams and blows on head

Child had a headache he was stripped and tied to bed

Child was begging he wanted a bun but nothing that morning he got

Child ride in a car AC music and smiles on face

Child was sent to school on foot after scolding

Child was begging crying to let go, the man did, but only as a game, to chase

Child was hit by a car he lay there, there was a wrapped
bun coming out of his, unfolding

Child came home to smiling to find his family death

Child that night when parents were at fight again hung
itself for life of his to end

Child was now strangled, his flesh was old, out of taste

Child could have been saved but he was three months too
late

And there She was

And there she was

Staring at me scared and lonely

Weak and fragile

Someone had hurt her not body but courage

Would she ever had be able to shine the world again with her smile

I could have maybe helped her

But something held me back

It was a false future, some weak bonds, little lack of courage and false truth I told myself

It was the honesty maybe that I lack

Beaten up and scared left alone given many names

She ran, she cried, she begged

And there she was

Asking me for help not her words just eyes

I am hurt too, hurt my self, killed something within

Who was I to define who she was

Who was I to decide what she deserved

Who was I not to shield her from nationalist

I was no one, I am no one

She did not wrote her reason, why

She did not explained her life to the world

Alone she was, else she had stayed a little while in this mad place

Photos in news, discussion in panels, relatives gatheredAnd there she was

Hanged to the ceiling

And there she left

The world with no feeling

No reason, why?

No explanation

She just ended her life

Not weak, no she was brave once, but it was before they killed her inner self

And now she is gone

Few days passed by

I saw a young angel
Tears she had, was crying red drops scared alone asking for
helpI blinked once

And there she was

Lost

What is Sense? Where is it hiding?

A thought, a question, a speed bump came to mind

How were we a few years ago? Are we same now?

Has something lost? Has something found?

Are we on right path? Or we are lost?

What is Sense? Where is it hiding?

They said we were free

To shut our eyes, shut our mouth, shut our thoughts, to shut our reasons

They said we have equal rights

To rape, to molest children, to steal and kill

What is Sense? Where is it hiding?

Silent and blind unite together

Independence for the ignorance, the irrationality, the religion

Children, women, mothers, sisters and daughters

Awaits in fear of being slaughter

Deaths of one true, the nature, in this place, the drama theater

What is Sense? Where is it hiding?

Rivers of blood is holy now

River of water is gutter

Every child belonged to religion

All cons runs our lives

Lies

It was a lie all along

I knew the reality but kept quiet

We all knew, no one stood to change our faith

But blinded ourself with moronic faith

It was a lie, a lie all along

Our freedom, the reality of unity

The meaning of love, the purpose of religion

Importance of money, the meaning of glory

Many things, maybe everything we were told may be was a
lie, a lie to be sold

To keep us quite, something was told

Everything is fine nothing will happens

Laugh, laugh hard, nothing here matters

Not even the children dying, women raped, sister sold

Nothing matter we are here just to play our role

Never knew, was told, never imagined otherwise

Never asked, was scared, follow the line

We are meant for money, never think otherwise

Would had jumped and helped those in need, but brother,
no time

It was a lie, a lie all along

A lie it was that we are meant for something

It was a lie that everything is fine

It was a lie that life is predefined

A bunch of lives burning the world in search of
something

What is the rights? And how free are we?

Are we not just soldiers in the blind army

Killing the trees, laughing at the burning lives

Slaughtering the sons and daughters of nature

Were we the same all along, the ignorant creature

It was the lie, the lie all along

God created humen,

Creating cancer for his own heaven?

There is a God looking at us,

Closing eyes of his when we die of torture rape and hunger

It was the lie, the lie all along

We should follow religion,

The teacher of discrimination, of ignorance

We should follow elders

A drunk man, a beaten woman, listen to them when they cut children's feathers

Blind we no more but still quite

Weak we no more but still scared

Alone we no more but can't unite

Ashamed yes we are, to try and fail telling people the truth

The truth is in the winds in ocean in the jungle

Truth is in us the truth we deny

Truth is in the little pleasure we get

The truth is the sorrow we felt

The truth is here right here

We know what is truth

But aren't we the brave sons and daughter scared

May be we are too selfish to think life out there

We are good, the best species on earth

With humble heart

Knowing how to love

Respecting the holy glorious farm dirt

It was a lie, a lie all along

No one came

No one came

No hand to help me

When I fell down

Only talking mouths and laughs

No one trusted

No one wanted to

My dreams trash for others

My life game for all

No one clapped

On my first dance

My first twirl, my first jump

Mumbling gossips and praying eyes

No one came to stop

In this men's world

When I was forced against the wall

Laughing men strong arms and blades

No one had guts

No one could stop me

They tried, the world tried, men tried

But failed and I laughed, I laughed

No one leaves their seats

No one can take eyes off me

I dance, I twirl, I jump

They clap, they cheer my name, and I, like always don't care

Somewhere

Somewhere in the middle

Between her and me

There is life we left behind

We ran away at last to be free

I didn't called her name

I didn't looked back for her

She has life now, her dream

I have mine, lonely empty I suffer

She had the most gorgeous smile

She had the best ways to make laugh

She had a heart desired to be loved

World would not move when she talk

Somewhere far in past memories

I still have her close to me

Her hairs are soft and voice melody

I regret what I left behind to be free

I was suffering before

But I had her with me

The world was small and dusty

But together, anywhere is best place to be

www.ingramcontent.com/pod-product-compliance
Lightning Source LLC
LaVergne TN
LVHW050423160726
843469LV00041B/1216

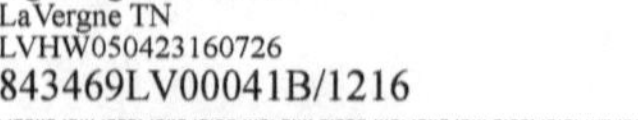